Memoirs fro

S.B.C

(The Sad Bastards Cafe)

By Michael Ross

To Sylvana,
A beautiful woman!
Thank you for bringing love &
laughter back into my life
Michael.
xx

ISBN: 9781549564628

LET ME TELL YOU

How this all started.

In 2005, my wife died suddenly and tragically.

Leaving me with 4 and 6 year old boys.

I was learning to get in touch with my 'feminine' side.

I was learning to shop for proper things like food, and essentials, not 'man' things like DVD's and games etc.

One day I noticed in a well known supermarket in Stockport, (I'm calling T.E) at one end, up one level was a cafe, part of a well known coffee shop chain, which I am calling (C.C), and I decided to have a break and sit up there and have a cappuccino.

The tables at the front , overlook the shop floor, so I had my coffee and sat at a table to glumly look over at the strange goings-on of the Stockport shoppers below.

Then I noticed , every other table had someone, glumly looking over at the shop floor drinking their coffees.

They all looked sad.

I did as well I suppose.

Hence the name - The **SAD BASTARDS CAFE! (SBC)**

SERIOUS DEDICATION

I dedicate this book to my 3 sons, Aidan, Benjamin and Oliver.

To my Brother, who insisted I went to the Doctor with prostrate problems, who discovered I had cancer, and after a Robotic Radical Prostatectomy by Mr Oakley, who saved my life, I am now fully cured.

To my lovely wife and sister, both up in Heaven, and all those who put up with my crummy jokes and over-bearing presence.

FUN DEDICATION

I also dedicate this book to all you **SAD BASTARDS** out there, who find themselves drawn to a famous cof-fee shop (CC) inside a well known Stockport super-store (TE)

Who can't help but watch the hapless, braindead, very typical Stockport shopper amble, trip, look, poke, point, handle, drop, deliberate, put it in the trolley, and stand and stare at it, take it out of the trolley, then put it back in, then out, and so on.

Ad infinitum.

ISBN: 9781549564628

CONTENTS

1 ANKLE ADORNMENTS

Why not kick these stories off with some simple photos that put it all in a nutshell!

ITALY -   Beautiful filigree woven gold anklet
SPAIN -   Hand crafted butterflies and charms
INDIA -   Diamonds and silver thread anklet
S.B.C   -   Typical electronic tag, so the police know where these shoppers are.

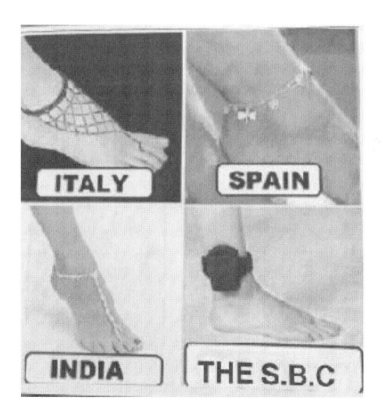

2 A DOG'S LIFE

Schhhhhhh!

I'm at the SBC.

Trying to catch the conversation of 3 young women
 at a table opposite.

Sounds very fruity, but only catching snippets of the
conversation.

These are the snippets I'm trying to put together, to
get the whole picture.....

"He's so lazy."

"He doesn't like to walk with me."

"He never listens to anything I say to him."

"He doesn't like to come for a walk when it's raining."

"He's snuggly when he gets into bed."

"His breath doesn't half stink sometimes."

"It's embarrassing when he starts scratching his bits."

"Yeah!" "Last night it was the worse ever!" "He was doing it right in front of my Mum!"

"And Mum was watching her favourite programme on TV, 'Dinner Dates', and had to leave the room!"

" He loves to come up to me and sniff me all over..it tickles!"

" He's caring , always likes to know I'm ok."

"I couldn't imagine life without him though."

OH FOR GOD'S SAKE!

GET TO THE HARD STUFF WILL YOU!

"He's got a boil on one of his testicles, he's going to

get it sorted out this afternoon."

WHAT??

"And while he's in there , he's getting his anal glands squeezed and cleared out."

YOU GOTTA BE JOKING!

What is wrong with people!

Hang on!

IT'S A DAMN DOG SHE'S TALKING ABOUT!

Well, I hope it is!

Drink your coffee and shut up Michael

3 SPOT THE SHOPPER!

The SBC will be open for business today.

A FREE coffee and an invitation to become an honorary Sad Bastard! (certificate supplied)

Today, as a one off, a prize will be given if you can spot a Stockport shopper who has more than 3 neurones in their head!

It won't be easy!

(clue : concentrate on those that have electronic tags strapped to their ankles/wear shell suits/are called Damien or Courtney)

See poor Fred on the previous page?

He has been on the NHS waiting list for 3 years to see a consultant about his irritating skin condition, he will be there!

I have met him there before...he has a very irritating habit of scratching his head and flaky bits of scalp falling in a constant stream into his coffee!

Never a dull moment at the S.B.C

4 "YEAH BUT, NO BUT"

So I'm back at the SBC

OMG!

The drama unfolded as soon as I took my seat in the cafe.

It was the loud raised voices.

Which became louder and louder and more urgent....

I couldn't at first see anything untoward?

But then again they have tall partitions between the aisles.

Suddenly, I saw what all the commotion was about.

A shoplifter.

Young. Tattooed. Stubble. Shell suit bottoms, hoody and? erm?

Yep, a girl!

I think?

Remember that girl in 'Little Britain' who kept saying "Yeah but, no but, yeah but, no but"etc?

This must have been her sister, maybe her clone.

She was running hell for leather, and fortunately her tatty trainers had good grip.
An assortment of items she had slipped under her hoody at the front and back were falling out, leaving a sort of paper trail.

I know we shouldn't laugh, but into view came two security guards.

They were of Caribbean origin, very large and round.

The bottom half of their shirts had un buttoned and become untucked from their trousers and were flapping around.

Breathing heavily, sweating profusely, they were trying

to catch "yeah but, no but."

Problem was, their standard issue T.E shoes had very smooth soles, and on the imitation marbled slippy T.E floor, they simply couldn't grip!

For all the effort, the grunting, the sweating they were putting in, they were travelling at 2 miles a fortnight!

No Mo Farrah smiles on these faces, oh no, you could see then sweat on their foreheads and feel the frustrations emanating from them in every direction.

At one point "yeah but, no but" stopped.

She had the audacity, and the time, to turn and give the security men the two finger salute!

And then, cool as a cucumber, turned and ran out of the store, all the while, bits of stolen T.E products, were still dropping out of the folds of her ample hoody....

The moral here is, if you have done something wrong, and suddenly face security who weigh twice as much as you and have slippy soled shoes.....RUN!

-

5 BUT WHAT IS IT ?

Ahhhhh!

It's half term of course.

All the little darlings are out in force, plus the
'I'm a mother and I'm going to breastfeed my baby in
public' brigade.

I'm all for that.

It's the most natural thing in the world, but why do
they have this immovable stare off face?

Almost challenging you to say something, but it's the
children running around that's making me nervous.

You see, when I was small, I was taught to behave, be
respectful and say sorry if I'd done something rude...

What happened?

It's the modern Mother's attitude of 'I'm having my coffee and nothing will disturb me while I faff around on my mobile', like Jonny, at a table nearby, smearing his bogey on a table, or Charlene, who has tipped her Mum's handbag all over the floor.

Now that IS interesting!

You see, men don't have any idea what goes on in a woman's handbag, what 'out of the world' items may be lurking inside.

The contents can make a Man's hair stand on end, to the point that a Man will keep his distance, as if whatever it is , is radioactive, dark and dangerous.

He will never reach forward to pick it up, touch it, in case he is infected by some sort of alien death plague.

THESE contents though, are compelling me to look, I'm being drawn in, in an altered hypnotic state....

Hmmmm.

I can see some anadin extra capsules, a small pack of tissues, some lippy, credit cards, purse, mascara, a tampax, half a packet of sweets...is that it?

Whoa!

Hang on!

Well now, what IS that???

Its small, pink and torpedo shaped.

It has, I think, a small opening for a battery?

(this is getting exciting, my breathing is getting quicker, my palms are sweating...)

So interesting, but what the hell is it??

I can see the blunt end has what looks like a ring of diamonte's around the bottom, but also grips to be able to twist and turn on?.

Now...let me see...a torch?

Nope, no bulb at the pointy end.

A drinks mixer?

Could be...but a little small.

This is SO intriguing

I'm not leaving here till I find out what it is..

Arghhhhh!

What happens next, happens in a flash and all at the

same time

1. Mum glances around , but does a double take, when she sees the contents are all over the floor

2. Mum shouts at Charlene

3. Mum jumps off chair to hastily shove all the contents back into her bag

4. Mum spots the small pink torpedo item on the floor. She freezes. The blood drains from her face. It had obviously fallen out of an unzipped pocket in her bag

5. She grabs the item very quickly, in doing so, somehow twists the end of the item, and suddenly it sounds like I'm being attacked by a swarm of bees!
   A vibration that goes to your very core. Conversation in the cafe has ground to an instant halt and everyone is rubber-necking to see whats happening.

6. Mum desperately tries to turn the thing off, all fingers and thumbs now, and in doing so, a flap at blunt end opens up, and out shoots this AA battery, which then, with speed, rolls towards my feet!

7. I step on battery to stop it rolling. We both look at each other. I reach down to pick it up to hand it to her

8. Mum has gone quite pink! She is stuttering, in a real flap, and starts to apologise, again and again.

9. Mr Stupid here, tries to help by lightheartedly saying " You will need this little battery if you want your...your...erm...little torch to light up"? "ha ha ha"

She laughs nervously, glances in an embarrassing way at everybody looking at her, scrambles everything together and off she goes, coat akimbo, child being dragged behind her.

Ah ha! I have figured out what the object is!

It's one of those battery operated cuticle removers or ear wax removers...I think?

If you think you know, pop your answer on a postcard , and send to the usual address.

Never a dull moment at the S.B.C.

6. NICE MELONS

Just back from Gateshead presenting a KETTFusion masterclass at Onebody4life, and thought I would call in at my favourite watering hole for a coffee.

Hello SBC!

Arghhhh! I saw a typically scruffily dressed Stockport shopper at the top of the escalator..oh, it's ok.

It's only a stuffed figure that T.E are using to promote some weird and wonderful product.

Uh huh?

What's wrong with the woman at the table next to me?

She is waving frantically at the shop floor…but I can't see anybody?

Now she is going crazy, standing, hopping, flailing her arms around like there is no tomorrow, whilst making strange squeaking noises.

I still can't see anybody?

Then she shouts out loud!

Ahhhhh! Got it!

It was a wasp!

And it must of stung her!

On the borders of her amply filled blouse it seems.

I thought about rushing over and offering some help?

Rub on or spay some antihistamine?

Even offer to suck the poison out?

Nope….I would have been accused of sexually harassing…and we wouldn't want that would we?

I have a reputation to uphold, even though my intentions are questionable but generally honourable.

It's such a shame nowadays that people do get the wrong idea if someone wants to help.

Anyway, I couldn't help but notice, as I looked down, she did have a beautiful pair of melons!.

My eyes couldn't help but wander over them, probably far too many times....

I mean, they looked beautifully ripe to me.

I wanted to check them

Run my hands over them, squeeze the ends with my fingers to see how ripe they were.

She obviously picked them up at the grocery section before coming up to the SBC

Might just get a pair of ripe melons myself to take home with me!

7 DEER STALKER

Well, my last visit to the SBC before my Spanish hols

Please don't disappoint me you Stockport shoppers!

But it's all feeling a little quiet here in the sanctity of the SBC

I notice already , not as many electronic tags on ankles, shiny chavvy track suits, pickpockets, loud mouthed kids running around, tipping trays of food upside down, smearing tomato sauce on table tops, swearing at the tops of their voices, and all the Mother does is shout at the top of her voice "For f**ks sake Tarquin, stop friggin running around"!

Even the very elderly, wrapped up as if they are on a

Smith's mystery coach journey to the North Pole, the men wearing their hand knitted Deer stalker hats, were nowhere to be seen

Deer stalker hats???

What IS that all about?

Have any of them even seen a live Deer?

They need to be informed that the chances of finding a live Deer in T.E, or indeed in the SBC, is very rare, never mind stalking a Deer

Stalking??

Even a packet of viagra couldn't help the old fogeys to stalk!

The elderly are simply nowhere to be seen.

Maybe they are off to Blackpool to ride the Pepsi max?

Well, it is the newest form of euthanasia.

Only 16% survive the shock of the first big dip!

Nope, everyone must be on their hols, curtesy of H.M prison at Strangeways.

Not much of a beach there though.

8 CAFE TRISTE DE BASTARDOS

Somebody today asked me, if I'm not at the SBC giving updates for 2 weeks, what will I do?

Simples, I will be sending updates from a little Spanish eaty/drinky place I know.

It's called the 'Solera'.

But of course, we will have to rename it for the purpose of continuity for all our SBC brethren.

Therefore, from henceforth, it will be called

Cafe Triste de Bastardos or CTB

So, from SBC to CTB, for the sake of the holidays.

Already some of you are asking -

Will the coffee taste the same in the CTB?

How do the Brits cope when ordering with their Manchester faux Spanish accents?

I will describe the looks on their faces when they order a full English breakfast and instead get a croissant and a cappuccino.

How they have done their best to order a plate of meaty kebab and instead been presented with a plate of barbecued marinated sardines.

The stunned looks on their faces when they are paying for a loaf of bread at the local supermercado, and they have to find 2 euros and 27cents, haven't a clue what the local dinero looks like, so they dump a handful of euro change on the lap of the Spanish assistant, and stand there with a look on their faces, reminiscent of one of the cast of 'One Flew Over The Cuckoo's Nest'

And the Spanish girl looks on them with absolute indifference and also pity, as if they are 6 year olds with learning difficulties…

Oh yes!

Bring it on

Hasta luego people

9 C.T.B - (CONTINUED)

I'm back here at the C.T.B

I like it here because this is a pit stop in the racy run of life, an oasis, to rejuvenate before the next semi-mad Stockport family comes along to create nervous ripples in the space time continuum

That's it!

Stockport shoppers are a race of brain dead aliens trying to integrate into the fabric of Human kind.

Although why the epicentre of this invasion had to be within the T.E, Stockport, escapes any reasonable explanation.

And sure enough, we have a typical alien Stockport shopper family at a table nearby.

Now, it might say 'English bacon and eggies' on the menu, but what arrives has a definite European slant to it

We have asparagus, in a light cheesy cream sauce, the bacon wafer thin, and, hells bells, not a whisper of toast and marmalade!

Well, this is a recipe for disaster with the Brit children.

"Mum"?, "What's this green plant doing on me plate?"

Mum says, "Oh, that's Asperges…er…Aspergusi…erm..Asaraguoso..erm..tastes a bit like broccoli..so just eat it and shut up!"

Hell child says, "I WANTS ME EGG N BACON!"

So he eats the toast instead, but the marmalade turns out to be apricot jam!

"UGH!", Hell child says, "I WANT MARMALADE!"

The Spanish waiter now sidles over, and looks at Hell child, like a matador looks at a bull!

"That IS marmalada!" he shouts

Now the tension is building up, I pretend to be anything but British, and I'm outta there before it turns into an international incident. Hasta luego!

10 "WHERE'S ME FRIGGIN i PAD"?

So it's my last few days on the Costa del Sol.

Im at a hand picked cafe, the C.T.B.

I have my cappuccino,

The sun is shinning,

I'm shaded underneath a leafy eucalyptus tree, and

the ambiance is cool, serene and calm.

Ahhhhhh!

"No!", "I don't know where your friggin i Pad is"

This came like a bolt out of the blue...

It's Mr and Mrs Stockport shopper and their 4.7 children walking out of the nearby Supermercado

How in the hell did they find my bolthole?

Is this karma for something I did in my previous life?

The whole family are arguing , in a very disjointed way, about completely different things…all at the same time

"Muuuum?",

"Those bites on me arm keep itching, what can I do"?

"Stop scratching them, how many times have I told you"?

"Daaaad?" "Me i Pad was in Mum's bag…but it's not there now"?

"Well, it's wherever you left it."

The boy trips and falls lightly onto the ground!

He doesn't hurt himself, so quick as a flash Dad says

"Ha ha ha", "Did you enjoy your trip Darren"?

Mum says to Dad, " Leave him alone won't you?"

To Darren she says " You alright luv?"

"I WANT ME i PAD"!

"I haven't friggin got it, right!"

Girl No. 2 says, "I want a wee"

Dad says "Wait till we we get back to the hotel, you can use the swimming pool like your Mum does"

Mum says "That's disgusting Bert!"

Dad says "What?" "You do it all the time." "I've seen you standing in there, then this stupid smile comes on your face."

Get the gist?

This is all happening as they amble, trip, and scratch as they come out of the Supermercado.

The semi-mad Stockport shoppers society are out everywhere…with their bright red backs, white bra lines on the top of their bright red shoulders, the tattoo's, the hairy legs, the hairy top lips, and women shorts that are 3 sizes too small, so it looks like play dough is oozing out everywhere…

HELP!

11 POT POURRI DARLING?

Ahhhhh!

In a strange weird way, it's good to be back in the SBC.

There is a deep seated connection, almost umbilical in its nature, that draws me back, that undoubtedly will take years of corrective counselling to undo

It's quiet!

Very quiet!

Too quiet?

Where is everyone?

I conducted a straw poll.

Well, I counted only 7 electronic tags on ankles, that means most of Stockport's infamous shoppers are still on holiday in Blackpool, Torremolinos, or stuck in a foreign airport terminal, because they are simply too drunk to be allowed on a plane, or even in re-hab… Yeah…Yeah…Yeah…, as the song goes!

I can hear a conversation between a middle aged couple underneath me on the T.E floor

The wife, resplendidly dressed in black, stained, see through leggings, that doesn't hide the fact that she is, how shall I put it, is hanging out, en mass, in ways that other beers cannot reach!

He still thinks he's on Blackpools Golden Mile, flip flops, manly stained shorts, and horrific 'grim reaper' tattoo's on the back of each calf.

The wife shouts at him, in a threatening uncultured way, "Bloody D***head!,". All I asked you to get was the double pack of the smoked back bacon, and you're here with a stinky pack of pot pouri??"

"Why??" She who must be obeyed commands!

By now , other shoppers have stopped in their tracks, pretending to look on the shelves, and men everywhere are sheepishly waiting to see how she is going to unleash her formidable womanly force.

He's standing there.

Quiet as a mouse.

Hardly breathing.

And then he takes courage and says, in a small diminutive voice…

"Erm…I thought it would make the house smell nice?"

For a second she says nothing, then her iris's change from a dirty grey to scarlet, her nostrils flare, she takes in a deep breath and says.

"Make the house smell nice?" she calmly says.

"MAKE THE FRIGGIN HOUSE SMELL NICE!"

You see I believe it was this poor man's way of coming out of the closet, of trying to connect with his feminine side.

We are all hoping his wife will treat this with the utmost sensitivity, with a caring attitude, what she says and does now has to come from deep within her heart, full of warmth and compassion.

"YOU F*ING T**T"!**

He holds his head down, and limps back to replace the item where it belongs.

No coming out of the closet today , my poor hen pecked friend!

Where are all the obnoxious children as well?

Has someone had the sense to conduct a humanitarian cull?

Oh no, there is a huge posse of them coming the wrong way up the escalator, leaving behind empty sweet and crisp packets, shouting, squealing, 'effing' and blinding etc

Don't worry about me.

All my inoculations are up to date, as I cut through the posse, with my pockets zipped to prevent straying hands.

Yep!

It's good to be back at the SBC.

12 HELL FISH

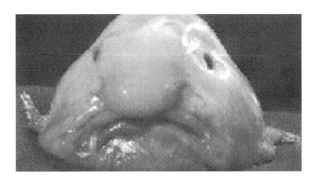

I love coming back to the SBC.

It's like an old glove, slightly worn and comfortable

A glove that you lost in the garden 15 years ago, and over time became buried in the sewage patch, so it's decomposed, been nibbled at by maggots, absorbed the grey sewage sludge that has slowly seeped out from a cracked sewage pipe nearby, and you have just unearthed it, covered in slugs, and decided to put it into the bin

People ask me, what does it take to become an honorary member of the SBC?

Well, anybody new are given tasks to complete, a coffee of their choice and are presented with a certificate on successful completion of the tasks.

One new novice had the audacity to request she could be a bona fide member of the SBC instead of just an honorary member..the cheek of it!

I like a nice piece of filleted plaice..so off I toddled to the fishmonger, we always start off with the same conversation.

"How big are the plaice today?"

" Ahhh," "A little small I'm afraid"

"Why?"

"Well the sea isn't cold enough"

"What??"

(I must point out, that the next part of this conversation I had with a fishmonger at a different branch of the T.E supermarket. My normal fishmonger is brilliant at his job. I've seen him skin and fillet an 18 foot great white shark in under 10 minutes)

Well, on this occasion, he said he had no filleted plaice left…but he had some whole plaice.

"Ok I said", "Can you fillet one for me please?"

Well, he squirmed, he broke out in a sweat!

You see, I know that the fish comes in filleted or not, and that SOME of the in-store fishmongers wouldn't know how to fillet a pineapple!

So he had a go, the poor chap, and when he was finished, it looked like a horrible deformed fish that must have been swimming in the waters next to a nuclear processing plant.

A bit of its tail was coming out of its left eye, and had a suspicious bulge appearing out of the left side of its body

He gave me a 50%discount.

And we both had a reet good laugh.

Lots of fun at the SBC.

13 STOCKPORT SHOPPER

Hello everybody!

The SBC calling

What is it with Stockport shoppers and warm weather?

As soon as that sun peaks out, its like an invitation to all Stockport shoppers to dress up accordingly, to amaze, to stun, always on the borderline of decency...

There is almost a weird carnival atmosphere.

It's very difficult not to stare, to stop your chin hitting the floor in disbelief, to stop yourself reaching for the sick bag.

And even the Guy's are at it

Look what one fella did, when the 1st rays of sunshine hit him when he walked out of the T.E supermarket, he whipped off his boxer shorts and wrapped them around the top of his head!

But that is life, and shows the humanistic diversity and the 'couldn't give a damn' attitude of our little North West population, known fondly as 'Stockport shoppers'.

14 DOCTOR SIR?

Yes!

I'm at the SBC again

As I left SSV (sports complex), the receptionist said,

"Off to the SBC?"

She knows me too well, and between you and me, she would be the perfect little sad bastard to join our dysfunctional club.

There are changes afoot!

Heck, the C.C and T.E are excelling themselves, not only clean sauce bottles on tables, but yes, actual sauce bottles in a tidy white carrier...

So I am enjoying my coffee and opposite is a Mother

with 2 children, with her little boy who can talk for England…which is great!

But there are worrying undertones.

He brandishes a pair of large plastic pliers, and recounts how he made his younger sister lie on his bed at home and then tried to execute a tooth extraction on her.

I'm turning slowly white. My heart is beating fast. Can it get any worse?

He then says he decided she needed ALL her teeth extracting!

Hells bells!

And all the while the Mother's giving me this fixed insane grin, like the Joker from a Batman film, but with far more lipstick on

I can tell she is a cultured Stockport shopper, because in an attempt to wipe her mouth after eating a cream cake, she has spread the thickly applied scarlet garish red lipstick half way up the left hand side of her face.

Back to the little nightmare standing facing me..sorry , I meant little boy, so then he brings out a plastic saw.

Arghhhh…..

It's got blood all over it!...hang on...it may be tomato sauce...well, I hope it is?

Anyway, his enthusiasm is running away with him, since he then says, "And then I wanted to saw Jessica's leg off!"

"Ha Ha Ha" I laugh nervously.

The tic in my left eye has come back, after years of not being there

What should I do?

Throw him over the edge of the C.C onto the Stockport shoppers down below on the shop floor?

Hell no!

They will probably eat him!

The Stockport zombie faction are out shopping today

Shall I carry out an exorcism?

Nope....if there is one thing that puts me off my donut, it's a child that can turn their heads 360 degrees!

No, I quickly drink my coffee and try to sneak out...

But no, quick as a flash, Damien (who I am now convinced is from the 'Omen') grabs my leg and tries to saw my leg off from the knee down!

I look to the Mother for help..but she just stares at me with that insane lipstick smeared immovable grin and says

"He likes you!"

So I give him my best cold intimidating stare…he let go for a sec…and I made my getaway.

I run back to my car shouting "I'm alive!" "I'm alive!"

15 MOTORISED MANIAC

I'm at the SBC

And, ha ha ha ha,…. I'm still laughing!

So I am in the bread aisle, and in front of me is an elderly lady in a very posh motorised wheelchair

(4 forward gears, 1 reverse, sat nav. and an ashtray)

I really don't think she can drive it!

It's huge

She is working her way down the aisle like a snow-plough driven by someone very drunk.

Weaving side to side and accelerating forward then braking suddenly..reminiscent of a dodgem car.

She has already rammed a trolly of bread a T.E employee was loading onto shelves.

The trolley was shunted forward.

Now the fun starts.

She shouts out "Sorry love, it's all new to me"

So she stops abruptly and puts it into reverse.

(yeah, yeah, it's also got reversing mirrors)

Eddie Stobart lorry drivers can reverse into a small gap with less than 6" either side.

But unlike those drivers, she is weaving the machine from side to side all the while gathering momentum.

But it was the piercing beeping of the reversing horn, that although she then stopped reversing, the horns didn't!

A baby started crying.

It was unbelievably loud!

People were falling over themselves to escape that aisle.

Suddenly the T.E immediate response team were there, in their fluorescent jackets, hard hats, tool bags and 1st aid kits.

What was funny was that they were shouting at the tops of their voices. In the middle of this, the lady in the wheelchair said the noise was making her feel nauseous!

Now, this was the conversation between themselves and the lady.

(T.E - the supermarket response team and E.L - Elderly lady in wheelchair)

TE - "Are you ok"

EL   - "All I wanted was some bread"

TE - "How do you turn the horn off?"

EL - "On Tuesdays"

TE - ???

TE - "Turn OFF the horn"

EL - "Who"

TE - "Can you hear me?"

EL - "What??"

TE - "I think there is a switch in a box under your seat, so let's turn it off?"

EL - "What??"

EL - "I think I am going to be sick!"

TE - "Oh God! Really?"

TE - "Shit!" "H-E-L-P!"

EL - "Yes....SICK!"

Anyway, an engineer with some pliers came and gave her the snip, the horn wires to the onboard speaker, and silence was restored.

We were all left with severe ringing in our ears, as if we had been to a Status Quo concert, with our ears pressed up against their speakers for 3 hours.

I made my getaway, as I was disappearing, I heard the horrible sound of someone being sick, poor lady, and as I looked around, I noticed one of the response team, legs akimbo, shooting up in the air, after she inadvertently stepped into the sick and was falling on her back, right into the middle of the mess!

Ahhhhh.

Never a dull moment at the SBC.

16 GAARDEN SPREENKLES

Well I'm here at the SBC.

Who would have thought it would take me 20 minutes to order my cappuccino?

No, it wasn't busy, I was served by a Lady from..from??

Not sure?

She started off by saying " Wat drink you?"

It went downhill from there

After 10 minutes of drawing a diagram of a cappuccino on a piece of tissue paper, pointing at menu's, pretending to drink out of a coffee cup, she cottoned onto the fact that I wanted a cappuccino.

Trouble was, by the end, the whole of the SBC was looking at me, as if I had some sort of major disability problem!

Jeeez!

How do you explain to someone , who only knows 3 1/2 words of English, what chocolate sprinkles are?

She offered me an unbuttered scone, some chips, a small packet of brown sugar.

God help me!

At last!

I saw a man bearing down on us that looked like a supervisor

He was definitely foreign looking, nothing wrong in that of course, but when I repeated my request for some chocolate sprinkles on the top of my cappuccino, he jumped in by saying "Gaaarden Sexy-ooon", and pointed towards aisle number 4 on the ground floor.

????

Eh?

????????

He said, in a very strange accent, "You wants garden for speeenkling?"

What?

I had to laugh at the absurdity of it all!

He saw me laughing.

He started laughing.

Then the lady who initially tried to serve me, who was lingering in the background all this time, also started laughing.

They laughed because I was laughing, as though they felt it was a strange British custom to laugh if someone else is laughing.

I laughed because he thought I wanted a garden sprinkler for my lawn (which is an artificial lawn anyway, and there was no way I was going to try to explain that)

So I bought my coffee, sorry, cold coffee by now, with a look like Eyore out of Winnie the Pooh, with no chocolate sprinkles on it.

I drank it in front of them.

And turned to leave, and as I did, they waved at me, still laughing!

????

Oh I do hope I have been a good enough boy this year for Father Christmas to bring me that luxury, leather hand stitched, KETTFusion embroidered straight jacket.

I feel I'm going to need to wear it when I next visit the SBC.

Happy (Bah! Humbug!) Christmas to you all!

17 OLD WOMAN

What ???

I'm here at the SBC for a lightening visit.

But it's almost full, with all sorts of undesirables.

Has there been a fire in the visitors section at Strangeways prison?

AND, all the balcony tables are full, and I can tell you, they are not all Sad Bastards!

It's disgraceful!

Don't they know those tables are reserved for Sad Bastards only?

And there are plenty of us, believe me!

Look?

No saucer for my coffee! No spoon!

Have they been stolen or waiting to be washed up?

The little old lady who serves the coffee is in a real flap!

One of her 6" false eyelashes has come unstuck, and hanging perilously on by a whisker (she has lots of those on her face)

She is wearing those very thick bottle end glasses, smeared with finger prints, that only the NHS could issue, and is cocooned in a haze of cuban cigar smoke.

I have focussed on that dangling eyelash, and I'm thinking to myself 'please don't drop into my coffee, pretty please?'

It would look like a drowning spider if it did, AND... oh hell, her wig has somehow moved to the right by 3" (She must have scratched her head and hasn't read-justed the wig) and now I can see the label on the side (do not machine wash)

Why do some people, usually men, wear dark coloured wigs, then sloppily allow tufts of white hair to sprout out from the side and back?

Some of her 3" thick foundation is visibly moving underneath…this is looking really freaky.

Her red garish lipstick, under pressure of her face movements, has extended sideways from the corner of her lips……

I wonder where Batman is?

Well?

I'm sure I'm looking at the Joker, re-incarnated now, after falling into a vat of boiling oil

Then she breaks my day nightmare and the air, with her raspy voice and looks me straight in the eye…

I wish I could do the same back, but she has a lazy eye, her left one as you look at her, which is winging it's way around her eye socket, after being magnified a 100 times because of the glasses, like a ball bearing in a pinball machine!

I want to shout out…"Please can you stop your eyeball for just 1 second!?"

But I feel it's too rude to say anything, and now I'm beginning to feel nauseous, so I concentrate on her other fixed eye, which seems to have an unnatural sheen to it? (I find out later, it's a glass eye) and she says "Scuse I, your coffee luv" and performs a wink (using the eye with the loose false eyelash) which I found very disturbing…

The only time I have seen a wink like that, where the whole face scrunches up, in a salacious semi-seductive way, was in a porno film called 'Snow White and the Seven Perverts'

I had a choice to come here today.

Bad choice.

Time for some more counselling.

See you later SBC.

18 TANTRUMS

I'm here at the SBC..again

I was right….most children are on half term

Funny, sales of tazers, strap restraints and straight jackets have rocketed up in price, its part of modern mothers war against tantrum children.

Your typical Stockport Mum wears a green bomber jacket with fake Mancunian fox fur around the collar, and jeans that looked like they had been attacked by Edward Scissor Hands.

There's more protruding white skin than jean material.

Uh oh! There's a commotion from the TE shop floor.

A Mum is pushing an overloaded trolley and there is a little girl, with scraped back pigtails in tow, who has decided to kick off!

Why do they do it in the most public of places?

She is now sitting on the floor, screaming at that pitch that can shatter crystal wine glasses.

The Mother , on the other hand, seems to be the epitome of calmness, trying to reason with her Daughter....and if you have ever had children...you just know that reasoning simply does not work!

The child, knows full well, she has got you by the short and curlies, and is tugging at her hearts content..compassion does NOT come into it.

But, you only have to look at the redness around the Mothers eyes to see what she is really thinking inside her head.

'WTF!' 'You little bitch!' 'Embarrassing me like this'. 'When I get you home, I'm going to slowly pull each and every one of your nails off with some pliers' 'I really want to throttle you here and now, but too many people are watching!'

The Mothers jawline is twitching, she is gnashing her teeth, and those BC years (before children) when she was in the army special forces interrogation unit, are going to come into play.

So, on the outside, with a frankly, demonic smile, she softly says, through gritted teeth, "Oh Darling," "Mummy loves you...you know that really!"

"Please stop making that awful screeching noise."

" I will get you that Princess Sparkle doll in the toy section."

"Then we can go home and have a lovely cuddle on the sofa."

Ha ha ha ... Little hell child knows this is a load of old bullshit, she can smell it in the air.

And her best bet and for the sake of her own safety, is to sit resolutely exactly where she is, screaming at the top of her voice!

This is the classic stand off.

The Mother stares daggers at hell child, hell child looks back, through the crocodile tears, straight into the eyes of the Mother, and knows she has got her Mother exactly where she wants her.

Suddenly the Mother moves, and quick as a flash grabs the little 'darlings' hand, and drags her on the floor behind her.

The girls screaming has suddenly reached fever pitch!

There is an old couple nearby, the lady shaking her head with sympathy for the Mother, the old gentleman, reaches for his hearing aids, face contorted in pain, since the screaming, if registered on a decibel meter, would show that the level is that of a jumbo jet taking off!

The loud 'squawking' feedback emanating from the hearing aids, adds itself to that of the screaming.

His wife, realising whats happening, shouts to him "Harry!," "Turn your hearing aids off!"

He says "What?"

She shouts louder "Turn your hearing aids off"

The hearing aids have also gone into meltdown and squawking even louder like a boiling kettle.

He says " Yes, it flushes well!"

His wife thinks "????"

Not realising, of course, he has already turned them off!

And so it goes on in a typical day at the SBC.

19 A FISHERMAN'S FRIEND

Ok.

Another quickie visit to the SBC

I'm going out on a limb. Daring to be different.

I wanted a honeycomb latte with extra special sprin-kles.

Boy, nobody is perfect…not even me…and very sym-pathetic to all disabilities, but facing me was someone who clearly had a severe hearing problem

I started off by ordering my choice at a normal vol-ume level.

But had to keep repeating it, louder and louder until he could hear it.

By now it is so loud, everybody in the whole of the SBC turned around to watch me.

They all had the wrong idea of course, they thought I was shouting, in an offensive way, at a poor disabled man who was deaf!

What was worse is that when he finally understood, he had to shout the order back at me…just as loudly??

Not just that, but also shouting, told me how much it cost, and he shouted as he counted out the change back into my hand.

Then when I thought he had finished, as I am sheepishly facing the hostile crowd, trying to explain with actions that I wasn't angry, just trying to get myself understood., the man behind the counter, shouted out, louder than ever, **"DON'T FORGET YOUR RECEIPT!"**. Which made me to jump a little and spill some of my coffee on the floor.

It's a damn good job I wasn't in a chemist, quietly waiting for my prescription of haemorrhoid cream to be prepared, then the same person shouting out across the heads in the chemist to me that it was ready.

"MR ROSS, THE HAEMORRHOID CREAM FOR THOSE NASTY PILES YOU HAVE IS READY!"

It slowly dawned on me, that everybody in the SBC then thought I was also deaf, because the man behind the counter was shouting!

I know that because I was now getting lots of sympathetic smiles.

I'm sure one woman mouthed the words "You alright luv?"

I thought, shall I go along with it and pretend I am an expert in sign language?

Trouble is, I only know one sign, and that one is Anglo Saxon, and even here in the SBC, would not have gone down well at all.

You see, I really popped in to get a little fun pressie for a colleague , a vivacious blonde friend, who is a personal trainer, and leaving to work on a cruise ship.

For the sake of anonymity, I shall call her 'Gertrude'

Now, I used to like to tease Gertrude on all things to do with the birds and the bees, she always reacts by going quite pink and laughing out loud.

So, I have chosen a card, and an ideal present, a packet of liquorish flavoured 'Fisherman's Friends'

Those dynamite little lozenges that can burn a hole in your tongue, but will cure any sort of chest infection, dengue fever and elephantiasis...

In the card, I composed the usual mush :

'That sea air can sometimes make you feel a little chesty, and if this happens, you will find this present will help'

'I promise you, once you have sucked a Fisherman's Friend, you won't want to suck anything else, and your chestiness will disappear !'

She will blush.

She will laugh out loud.

I am naughty aren't I?

Mission done and dusted…and that new latte was delicious, well, what was left in the mug, after spilling half of it on the floor when I had jumped previously.

The musical strains of 'Captain Pugwash' were swilling around my head as I made my way down from the SBC, across the whole shop floor of the TE, and back to my car in the car park.

20 CHEAP BOXERS

I'm at the SBC with good friend, ace receptionist and conveyor belt baby factory, Hermione (I've changed her name for privacy)

Jennie (Ooops!) has brought along her youngest 'Brat' (her words, not mine), who is lovely!

So we are there enjoying our coffees, along with all the other sad bastards, and I noticed Jennie, out of the corner of my eye, eyeing up one of the Costa coffee 'baristas'.

She will vehemently disagree of course...

You see, these 'toy boy Latin' types, will insist on wearing moth eaten jeans that are always 2 sizes too large, and as a consequence, end up half way down at the back to the backs of the knees, with their multi-coloured boxers, oops, actually I think they were originally white, but they are now a little dirty from wiping their rear ends , like a mop, across dirty tables.

They have, clearly marked, the tell tale brand name across the elastic band keeping them up, but unfortunately, where one would expect to see Kalvin Klein, Boss, etc…instead we have 'Poundland Xmas Special', in bright red letters, and he has jet black hair that looks like it's dripping with oil.

I'm sorry , but it shouldn't fool any woman, but, one latin seductive look, and Ladies are melting onto the floor.

Lets go back to those untouchable boxers.

I'm sorry. They looked cheap!

Probably don't have an opening on the front…

Maybe only one on the back?

Or maybe he put them on back to front?

Who knows.

Anyway…

After our chinwag and catch up, I continued with my shopping.

I wanted some Christmas tree lights.

I could see 7 varieties of lights draped around a display.

I asked the assistant, for a set of the 'C' lights.

She said " We ain't got none!" "They sold out"

I said, "Please could I have the set of lights off the display?"

She said "Oh no…it's against company policy, they are there to help promote and sell the lights"

I said " But you don't have any lights left?" "So if you don't have any of those lights left, why advertise them, when you can't supply them?"

Hah! How could she possibly argue with that simple logic

She looked at me, straight in the eye, and with a big condecending sigh said " Because my section leader says so, so there!"

Hmmm. There was no appealing to her logic, sense of fairplay, Christmas spirit etc

So came home and sat and stared at our Christmas tree, looking like it was lodged on the dark side of the moon… Bah Humbug!

21 HAPPY PERVI XMAS

Another quick visit to the SBC

Is it Christmas overkill or what?

And why do the promotions for this Christmas follow almost on the heels of last years promotions?

Yep, the aisles are full of Christmas crap

The staff of the T.E are dressed up with knotted jumpers, even more 'scratchy' than the type your Grandma used to knit for you

Some wear floppy red hats or deer antlers that blink.

Some of them flash!

(No, not the staff, the costumes they are wearing)

"Press me here!" said one member of staff who crept up behind me and scared me half to death

He looks like a serial killer, he had those eyes that you have seen on condemned men ready to walk the green mile, that are simply set worryingly, far too close together in their face.

'What??" I say, whilst stumbling back.

"Press me here, here, come on, press it now!"

Phew!

I think he meant the rather bulbous 'Father Christmas' nose on this thick woolly stained jumper.

So, tentatively I did, if nothing else other than to make him go away..please?

As I did, the 'nose' said in a loud, breathy , raspy voice "Ho! Ho! Ho!"

Eughhh!

THERE WAS SOMETHING STICKY AND WET ON HIS JUMPER!

Why were the hairs on the back of my neck standing up?

But it was the look on his face that bought back that

tick I used to have in my left eye.

I was going into a cold sweat, a panic attack, I wanted to run hell for leather!

His eyes narrowed, and he was uttering this weird serial killer giggle

"My friend, don't you think this is funny?"

Problem was, that when he spoke to me, a minute speck of spit shot out of his mouth and hit me just under my right eye!

I was now transfixed!

I was doing an involuntary manikin pose.

I wanted to wipe it away.

Disinfect it with some domestos, and scream out loudly.

But my middle class upbringing meant I waited there like an absolute idiot, feeling the spit slowly dry under my eye!

As if nothing has ever happened.

Why do things like this always happen to me?

I stumbled and ran to the car, feeling as if that 'alien', from the film 'Alien', had jumped out of his stomach and transfixed itself across my face.

I have some disinfectant wipes in the car, I tore one out, and after vigorously scrubbing for a couple of minutes, and felt almost normal again.

Jeez!

Some visits here can turn into your worse nightmare.

Back to counselling.

22 CREATIVE COFFEE

The octogenarian lady who serves the coffee in the SBC, the one with the mahoosive false eyelashes, one of which is always teetering, threatening to fall in one's coffee while she is preparing it, and the candy floss hair that is sculptured into a mountain on the top of her head, so it resembles the mountain in the Spielberg's film 'Encounters of the 4th Kind', and who's top set of false teeth rattle around her mouth as if they are solar powered, has excelled herself today.

The design on the top of my coffee is unbelievable!

How she can do that with shaking hands, where a semi landslide of hair has fallen down and fused with the glue from her left eyelash, so when she blinks, only her right eye closes, only beggars belief.

It's a piece of art!

Beautiful!

And even the way she manages to retrieve a bunch of broken hairs that fell in the coffee when the landslide from the rest of her piled up hair was happening, without destroying the design, blows me away.

This has put me into a great frame of mind for some more hols of mine in Spain in a few days time.

Don't worry Sad Bastards, I will be reporting from the Spanish equivalent, 'Cafe Tristes de Bastardos' or CTB for short.

We have played this game before, haven't we readers, in an earlier chapter?

Go on, shout it, with feeling, with bravado, with intent tinged with anger, spit it out!

B-A-S-T-A-R-D-O-S!

Feels good doesn't it?

Of course it does!

Anyway, I believe now, and it's taken years for the penny to drop, that I have been condemned by the cosmos to know that wherever I go in the world, I will be surrounded by Stockport shoppers.

It's my karma playing out for something terrible I must have done in a previous life.

Maybe Spielberg can produce and direct a new film entitled 'Stockport Shoppers of the Worse Kind'...

I'm sure it was be a massive blockbuster!

He wouldn't be able to Hollywoodise it though...oh no...no perfect smiles, no personal limousines for transport, no luxury trailers filled with Perrier water, no make-up dolly birds...

It would have to be 'What you see is what you get', a tram at end of the day, and a smelly little caravan parked in the public car park, a ploughman's lunch with optional pickles, oh yes, Stockport shoppers are the salt of the earth, oh yes, even though it's been spread on roads, swept up, mixed with sand, melted, swept up again and stored in hangers at various points on the M60.

23 THE BALLOON

I'm settled in my favourite seat, overlooking the shoppers from the SBC

My God!

It's busy?

Arghhhhh!

Just remembered , more school holidays again

And immediatly I am trapped up here...

There are children everywhere.

Like the one facing me now.

He's around 8, a council estate face with a

permanent scowl.

His bleached hair is sticking straight up, probably coated with 2 gallons of extra strong wallpaper glue.

He has loose fitting dirty jeans, and even sports a 'builders butt crack!'

He approaches me with a fresh deflated balloon, not a small one by any means, it's bright red and already, before any air has been blown in, is 1 1/2 foot in diameter.

"Blow my balloon up!"

"And the magic word is?" I say

"Fool!" He says, quietly, with a very strong Stockport council estate accent

"Fool?" I say.

"YES!" This time he is shouting.

"BLOW MY BALLOON UP....FOOL!"

(as he says this, he gets louder and louder, he's gone red in the face, and looks as though the blood vessels on his neck are going to explode)

Now, I'm not normally lost for words, although 2 did pop up (all to do with going forth and multiplying)

Even I wasn't going to say them out loud, so I

mouthed them through gritted teeth.

He shouted even louder.

"FOOL!"

Now it seemed everybody was looking at us, even the zombie's from the shop floor strained to look up to the SBC

Where the hell was his Mother?

Did he even have one??

Ahhhh Yes. Next table along, staring me down.

She let out a big sigh, and started laughing to herself, so hard in fact, thought she might have dislodged the electronic tag wrapped around her ankle.

"Get your arse over here Damien, leave that old man alone!"

Now THAT was below the belt!

Time for retribution.

'Let me have that balloon" I said, ever so gently, with a smile reminiscent of Hannibal Lector in 'Silence of the Lambs' when he meets Clarissa for the first time.

I started to blow the bloody thing up, I was getting light headed, but kept blowing, blowing , blowing.

Finally, it was huge.

Damien looked very pleased with himself.

Now, at this point, I decided not to tie it off.

Oh no!

As I went to hand it to Damien (and timing was going to be essential here) and just before his grubby little fingers grabbed it....

I LET GO!

It 'farted' it's way across the ceiling of the SBC, came back on itself, and then shot over the edge and down towards the shop floor of the TE

Round and round it went.

Up and down it went.

In and out it went

And eventually laded on the head of one of the Managers having an impromptu meeting in the Veg section

The manager was acting as though he had been attacked by a giant hornet, flapping away at the top of his head, legs stomping up and down.

Everybody in the SBC, including the little possessed one's Mother, watched the maiden flight of the farting red balloon.

In the middle of this , Damien was transfixed, his mouth wide open!

I made my getaway.

As I was half way across the shop floor , to the exit and car park.

I could hear him starting to kick off!

Shouting, thrown coffee cups etc.

I walked out of the TE, with a spring in my step, prancing along as if I was in a dressage competition, with the biggest self-satisfied smile I have ever worn.

Oh sometimes, just sometimes…

 I love the SBC!

24 THE LEASH

It's been a while since I have visited the SBC.

Today Boy's and Girl's …it's story time!.

Once upon a time there was a frazzled Mother.

Who looked and walked around like Eyore from Winnie the Pooh.

As she slowly ambled along the aisles of the T.E, she was connected by a garish multicoloured nylon fabric leash to a little toddler, dressed up as a T.Rex!

He was trouble!

Trouble was emanating from him in all directions, you couldn't actually see it. You could only feel it. Invisible radioactive-like waves, plus of course, the slight whiff of a soiled nappy.

I'm sure he looked like he had the numbers 666 tattooed on the left hand side of his temple?

Bet he was called Tarquin or Damien.

He had nearly chewed his way through the nylon leash that was stopping him from bringing uncertainty and destruction to the population at large.

As shoppers were approaching him, they were quickly veering away to one side, as if he was a rabid dog!

The leash was very long.

Too long.

Which meant that he reached the liquid washing machine detergents before his ambling Mother rounded the corner of the aisle...

He focussed on a very large pink bottle of Comfort, he easily unscrewed the top off, and stuck his nose into the large opening , while gripping the bottle with both hands.

He shoved his nose too far in which made him sneeze, and at the same time, the bottle slid quickly out of his hands and hit the floor right way up, but with force.

A pink column of Comfort shot two foot into the air

and splashed onto the floor all around him, but not one drop on him?

It spread slowly, as if in slow motion, in an ever increasing circle around him.

His Mother/carer/trainer/exorcist reacted way too slowly to have prevented any of this.

Suddenly, a T.E employee came running to the rescue, armed with a bucket and mop which was clattering left and right.

The Gentleman was foreign, and was shouting out loud "Not to Vorry!" "Not to Vorry!"

Next second, there was a silence, as he shot up in the air and landed flat on his back.

All the air in his lungs shot out, I'm sure I could smell garlic?

A combination of a very slippy spillage and shiny soled standard issue T.E black shoes, meant the only way was down!

The devil child, sorry, toddler, opened his mouth and laughed out loud (I'm sure he added another load to the deposit he had already squished into his nappy)

"Again!" "Again!" the toddler kept shouting.

The man, as he slowly tried picking himself up, then

slipping down again, then picking himself up, then slipping again…well, you get the gist…

The man said something very foreign.

It didn't sound very pleasant.

And I bet it didn't translate as :

"Oh, what a beautiful day"

or

"Oh, fiddlesticks"

or

"Oh, these things happen" "Ha Ha"

or

"Oh, I do love that little boy's laugh"

Suddenly the other end of the leash appeared and then the leash holder said

"Come along Cadogan"

Cadogan! Cadogan?

Did she mean Cardigan??

God only knows!

Anyway they dissapeared. The foreign Gentleman was still muttering garlic flavoured profanities under his breath as he was cleaning up, all the while, he was concentrating keeping his legs from slipping under him...have you ever seen a Giraffe spread their legs to drink water?

The Mother and toddler were making their way up to the SBC, and it may have been possible that they all lived happily ever , AFTER, Concrete Mixer? erm...I mean Cadogan, had eaten his way, finally, through the whole of the nylon leash holding him back from attacking and causing mayhem with the unsuspecting walking dead, known affectionately as Stockport Shoppers.

25 HORSEY BUSINESS

As I walk into the T.E, I couldn't even reach the escalator to take me up to the SBC, when I was confronted by a wild banshee!

A woman, wearing jodhpurs, hair scrawped back into an untidy ponytail, hands full with all sorts

She was running full pelt towards the tills.

Now, there is that awkward moment when neither of us knew which side of me she was going gallup past

To the left? To the right?

This was **NOT** going to be a classic **NASA** docking manoeuvre.

No Sireeee!

I sidestepped to one side.

The wrong side.

As we collided, there was a confabulation of arms, legs, bits of horse manure from the woman's jodhpurs, and most of what she was carrying , shot up in the air and then for an infinitesimal moment in time, hung there, then clattered onto the floor around us.

But...

It ended with a large plastic pack of ripe 'tomatoes on the vine' being catapulted 6ft into the air, just as she landed on top of me!

So the tomatoes in slow motion, started to descend and hit the floor near our heads, the pack split open and the tomatoes shot off in all directions.

She shouted , very loudly, in my left ear "SHIT!"

It's been a very long time since a woman has shoved her ample 36 double D into my chest.

I smiled and said instantly "We shouldn't keep

meeting like this!"

She seemed to linger for a nanosecond, like we were in treacle, but then we both picked ourselves up and dusted ourselves down.

I had an impulse to offer to dust down her 36 double D's, but, decency said, 'No you perv!'

She smiled nervously, went bright pink, and rushed off, never to be seen again.

She left me with the very faint smell of horses on my arms and chest.

Ahhhhhh!

The SBC…Always full of surprises.

26 DRESSCODE?

He wrote: "Please can you put a rule in place that people like this will not be served in your stores. It's bloody disgusting."

Whats all the fuss about?

Stockport shoppers shopping at the TE and having a coffee in the SBC....in their PJ's?

It's what happens

Wake up!

And thats just the start of it.

It's what makes the world go round.

It's what makes Stockport shoppers who they are

At the cutting edge of bad taste..and this is just the tip of the Stockport shoppers bad taste iceberg...check these out :

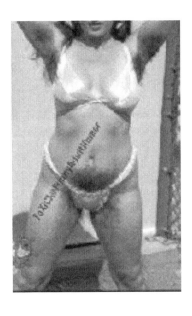
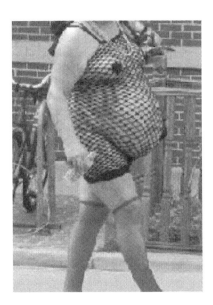

27 HOT DOG MADAM?

Ok...

Everybody keeps asking me why I am a little conde-
scending about the Stockport shoppers who frequent
the T.E and the CC within the SBC.

(I will wait while you put your false teeth back in after
that tongue twister)

Why do I make fun of them?

Look, for example, if I gave you a hotdog with a little
mustard on it, how would you eat it?

Yes, of course you would, you would hold the blunt
end to your lips and nibble away until you came to the
other end.

Then wipe your lips with the tissue you held the hot dog in..right?

Hah!

Not so your typical 'Stockport shopper'.

Oh no!

First of all they would eat the bread roll on it's own.

Then they would have to toss the sausage in the air and try to catch it in their teeth, while their hands were behind their back, and try to swallow it whole!

But they can't.

Because they have no coordination!

The photo at the top of the previous page says it all.

But there is another aspect to all this.

It's pride!

Pride in being different from the norm.

Stockport shoppers dare to be different, even if they do have hot dog juice dribbling down their chin and smell of Coleman's French mustard.

28 THE BANDWAGON

Whats all this?

Following on from the phenomenal success of the SBC, other usurpers to the crown are vying to be a part of us.

The SBC is sacrosanct.

It's a place where you can meet, to discuss the world, life and anything in the universe.

To be an Honorary Sad Bastard for an hour, you will leave rejuvenated!

Your road rage will reach new heights!

Your attitude to traffic wardens will reach new lows!

But hey, there is an organisation we think could benefit us, in a symbiotic way, it's fantastic news really.

We are going into partnership with the Cafe Penis, on the Rue de la Penis in Paris.

Check out the photo on the other side of this page.

See that girl?

She's been searching for a 'Penis' for a very long time, and finally she found one.

It's not that big, but does she care?

No way Jose!

Look at the way she's jumping for joy!

That what happens now when strangers finally find the S.B.C.

They jump into the air.

Problem is, they miss the handles of their zimmer frames when they finally come back down to Earth.

The surrounding Stockport shoppers always show their sympathy by laughing very loudly!

29 DO YOU HAVE THE 'STOCKPORT SHOPPER' GENE?

Ladies and Gentlemen, this is a very simple test to determine whether or not you would be classified as a 'Stockport Shopper'.

Read then look at this photo.

If a smile does not appear on your face within 3 seconds, I'm afraid you may be a Stockport Shopper.

The ability to recognise something humorous takes a higher intellect, something that the Stockport Shopper gene inhibits.

After recent poll at the T.E, carried out over a 7 day period, of 3,457 people during peak times, in the 2nd week of June, 2017, it was determined that over 97% of people in this area, had the 'Stockport Shoppers' gene.

No amount of treatment, chemical , psychological or otherwise, can permanently remove that gene.

There are varying degrees of 'afflictions' that this gene causes.

If you display any of the following, you must go immediatly to your nearest 'Stockport Shopper' counselling centre.

1. Wanting to wear unusual make-up, and couldn't care less if people laugh at you.

2. Have frequent bouts of road rage when driving

3. Trying to drink yourself stupid at home with red wine, cava or lager, and posting it on Facebook.

4. To constantly claim your partner never listens to you

5. To get yourself all worked up, waiting for the New Year sales, so you can fight, scratch and spit to get your hands on that pashmina jumper which was reduced to half price.

6. To feel obligated to visit the Manchester Xmas markets, to drink too much gluhwein, and complain that the cold rain should be snow and finally whinge that it's all way too expensive compared to last year.

7. To take photos of your dog, fast asleep on its back, stark bollock naked, or a plate of mushy food, and post it on Facebook, in the misapprehension that the rest of the unsuspecting public really want to see it?.

8. Complain incessantly about having to get up for work, the traffic jam to work, work itself, your work mates, the journey home from work and finally arriving at No. 3 (see previous page)

9. This only applies to women in their 40's and 50's. They reach a stage where they try to apply make up as if they are only 16! It certainly doesn't fool anyone. And certainly here in the North West, is known as looking like 'mutton dressed up as lamb'.

Finally, let me introduce you to the team that is out there helping, annoying, cajoling, sympathising and trying to save all the newly discovered 'Stockport Shoppers'.

These are people that have the dreaded gene themselves, but have learned to live with it.

That doesn't mean they won't be displaying all the traits associated with the gene, and in fact, a 'Stockport Shopper' can identify themselves with them much more easily. and because of it, are more approachable.

On the next few pages, we have :

1. Grizzle

2. Maria Imaculatata

3. Cross Eyed Suzie

and last , but not least, our illustrious Director of

Operations :

Bert.

GRIZZLE : Genuinely wants to help, but does have serious issues with his people skills. One look into his eyes is normally enough to calm someone who has had a serious 'Stockport Shopper' episode. Apparently, I have been told, he looks like he is going to slit your throat!

MARIA IMMACULATATA : From Spain originally, was working in the SBC as a waitress when she contracted a virus that altered her genes, and in a short space of time became a 'Stockport Shopper'.

Her accent is atrocious, but her right hook legendary.

Long before the SBC, she was with a travelling circus, and could sharpen the knives, the knife thrower uses for his act, using the rough bristles on her legs.

CROSS EYED SUZIE : Actually from Stockport. Loves to be the centre of attention, but goes apeshit if you laugh at her cross eyed affliction.

She also has a problem with her lips, that go into spasms when she is anxious

Also worked in the SBC at one time, but kept placing trays on the wrong table, thinking she was putting them on the right one (again, all to do with her crossed eyes)

BERT :

Our Institute Director. She has the full blown unexpurgated 'Stockport Shopper' gene. As you can see, it manifests itself particularly, in her case, in what she likes to wear.

This is very typical dress for a 'Stockport Shopper'.

She has a heart of gold, and will do her best to cough on you, pinch you, trip you up, and show you how to shop for the most ridiculous items known to man.

ABOUT THE AUTHOR

Michael Ross

Lounge lizard, all-round sportsman.

Jolly good egg.

God's gift to women (in his dreams)

Loves to make people laugh.

As generous as hell.

Lives life to the full.

And his motto?

'Make the most of this life.

Because we don't get out of it alive!'

19453383R00074

Printed in Poland
by Amazon Fulfillment
Poland Sp. z o.o., Wrocław